Animals and Their Senses

# ANIMAL TOUCH

by Kirsten Hall

Reading consultant: Susan Nations, M.Ed.,
author/literacy coach/consultant

WR WEEKLY READER
EARLY LEARNING LIBRARY

**Please visit our web site at: www.earlyliteracy.cc**
**For a free color catalog describing Weekly Reader® Early Learning Library's list**
**of high-quality books, call 1-877-445-5824 (USA) or 1-800-387-3178 (Canada).**
**Weekly Reader® Early Learning Library's fax: (414) 336-0164.**

**Library of Congress Cataloging-in-Publication Data**

Hall, Kirsten.
  Animal touch / Kirsten Hall.
    p. cm. — (Animals and their senses)
  Includes bibliographical references and index.
  ISBN 0-8368-4806-3 (lib. bdg.)
  ISBN 0-8368-4812-8 (softcover)
  1. Touch—Juvenile literature.  I. Title.
  QP451.H15   2005
  573.8'75—dc22                    2005046172

This North American edition first published in 2006 by
**Weekly Reader® Early Learning Library**
A Member of the WRC Media Family of Companies
330 West Olive Street, Suite 100
Milwaukee, WI 53212  USA

Copyright © 2006 by Nancy Hall, Inc.

Weekly Reader® Early Learning Library Editor: Barbara Kiely Miller
Weekly Reader® Early Learning Library Art Direction: Tammy West
Weekly Reader® Early Learning Library Graphic Designer and Page Layout: Jenni Gaylord

Photo Credits
The publisher would like to thank the following for permission to reproduce their royalty-free photographs:
AbleStock: 8, 17, 18; Brand X Pictures: 19; Corel: 21; Digital Vision: cover, title page, 6, 7, 12, 13, 16;
EyeWire: 9; Fotosearch/Brand X Pictures: 20; Fotosearch/Corbis: 4, 10; Fotosearch/Digital Vision: 15;
Fotosearch/Goodshoot: 11; Fotosearch/image 100: 5; Fotosearch/SuperStock: 14

Printed in the United States of America

1 2 3 4 5 6 7 8 9 09 08 07 06 05

## Note to Educators and Parents

Reading is such an exciting adventure for young children! They are beginning to integrate their oral language skills with written language. To encourage children along the path to early literacy, books must be colorful, engaging, and interesting; they should invite the young reader to explore both the print and the pictures.

*Animals and Their Senses* is a new series designed to help children read about the five senses in animals. In each book young readers will learn interesting facts about the bodies of some animals and how the featured sense works for them.

Each book is specially designed to support the young reader in the reading process. The familiar topics are appealing to young children and invite them to read — and reread — again and again. The full-color photographs and enhanced text further support the student during the reading process.

In addition to serving as wonderful picture books in schools, libraries, homes, and other places where children learn to love reading, these books are specifically intended to be read within an instructional guided reading group. This small group setting allows beginning readers to work with a fluent adult model as they make meaning from the text. After children develop fluency with the text and content, the book can be read independently. Children and adults alike will find these books supportive, engaging, and fun!

— Susan Nations, M.Ed., author, literacy coach, and consultant in literacy development

People touch with their skin. **Nerves** in our skin carry information about what we touch to our brains.

The tips of our fingers have many **nerve endings**. They help us know whether something is hard or soft, hot or cold, smooth or bumpy, or wet or dry.

A raccoon's front paws have thousands more nerve endings than human fingers do.  Raccoons can find food in the dark or underwater just by touching it.

Most frogs have a very good sense of touch. Frogs feel objects with their fingertips, too.

A spider has small hairs on its eight legs. The hairs help a spider feel objects move and movements in the air when **prey** is nearby.

whiskers

The long stiff hairs on a seal's face, called **whiskers**, can feel movements in the water.  The whiskers help the seal catch fish even when the water is dark.

Cats use their whiskers like feelers.
Whiskers help cats know when objects
are close to them, especially in the dark.

tentacle

Snails use their bottom **tentacles** to feel their way around. They also use these tentacles to taste and smell.

trunk

Some animals touch each other to say hello. Elephants greet each other by rubbing their trunks together.

Some animals touch each other to be helpful. Monkeys use their fingers to clean each other's fur.

Many animals use touch to show caring.
Giraffes show caring by touching each
other's noses.

Sometimes touching can hurt!
Kangaroos hit and kick each other
when they are fighting.

Polar bears sit, walk, and sleep on snow and ice. A polar bear's body is covered with thick fur that helps keep the bear from feeling the cold.

Penguins swim in cold water and walk on ice and snow. A penguin's body has a thick layer of **blubber**, or fat, that helps keep it warm.

Many animals live in very hot places. Desert lizards have long legs that help keep their bodies from touching the hot sand and rocks.

A camel's knees, elbows, and chest have pads of thick skin. The pads let the camel lie down on the hot sand.

Orangutans use touch to comfort their young.  A young orangutan stays with its mother for seven or eight years.

Animals use their sense of touch in
many ways.  Touch helps an animal
learn about where it lives.

# Glossary

**nerve endings** — the tips of nerves

**nerves** — thin, stringlike parts that carry messages between the brain and other parts of the body

**prey** — animals that are hunted and killed by other animals for food

**tentacles** — long, bendable parts that stick out from the heads of some animals

# For More Information

## Books

*Amazing Animals.*  Rookie Reader (series).
Betsy Franco (Scholastic)

*Animal Senses.*  Etta Kaner (Sagebrush)

*Animal Senses: How Animals See, Hear, Taste, Smell
and Feel.*  Pamela Hickman (Kids Can Press)

*Touching in Living Things.*  Senses (series).  Karen Hartley,
Chris Macro, and Philip Taylor (Heinemann Library)

## Web Sites

Wacky Whiskers Quiz
*www.nationalgeographic.com/ngkids/9706/wackyq.html*
A quiz about how animals use their whiskers

## Index

## About the Author

**Kirsten Hall** is an author and editor.  While she was still in high school, she published her first book for children, *Bunny, Bunny*. Since then she has written and published more than eighty titles. A former teacher, Kirsten currently spends her days writing and editing and her evenings tutoring.  She lives in New York City with her husband.